VOICES OF NATURE

LOVE, MOTHER EARTH

FIRST EDITION

Published by
Wild Horses Press
https://www.racqueltw.com/books

Editor: Nate Scott
GreatNateScott.com

Cover Design: Timothy J. Tri
TimothyTristan.com

Author Photography: Pete Carter
pjcarterimaging.com

Published in the United States of America

Print ISBN: 978-1-954539-02-0

DISCLAIMER

All contents in this book are for entertainment purposes only. It is recommended you consult with your spiritual or religious advisor, or licensed medical doctor. If you do anything suggested in this book, the publisher and the author, distributors and bookstores, present this information for entertainment and information purposes only. This book presents the author's thoughts; opinions, feelings, experiences and you are responsible if you choose to do anything based on what you read or the writing exercises.

For you and you alone

CONTENTS

INTRODUCTION TO RACQUEL TW

Racquel TW is a native to Los Angeles and is of Apache and Chumash Native American, Mexican, and European descent. She had the privilege of holistic living being passed down from her ancestors and considers it a sacred honor and privilege. Because of their love and culture, she was able to feel the connection to them in all things regardless of them being on Earth or with the stars.

The magic of words has always been prevalent in Racquel TW's life. Her mother read to her avidly everyday as a child, so it was natural that when she could on her own that she read voraciously everyday also. Her grandmother echoed these sentiments and they would all get lost in bookstores and libraries. She and her three siblings would have "sleepovers" in her room and tell each other stories with their stuffed animals. During lunch she and her friends would tell one another scary stories on the school benches around a favorite shady tree. The enchantment on their faces lit her soul up when telling stories. Getting lost in her imagination while reading her favorite books, going into a different and magnificent world, while being still, she knew that words were powerful.

She began to write poetry consistently at the age of 13, subsequent to beginning her Reiki practice at age 12 alongside her families' passed down spiritual traditions. These practices kept her grounded during a tumultuous period of her personal and family life. Always keeping a diary from the moment she knew how in elementary school, but it was during this period that her journal entries began to take on the form of poetry. Surprised to see what was coming out of her she noticed the cathartic effect it had on the emotions she felt she was alone in having. Her journal was her confidant, therapist, and cheerleader. The poetry itself was her gift during the darkest moments of her life. Never imagining sharing it with anyone, in spite of her knowing they were something special. Until she was inspired to share them with her best friend, whose response was enthusiastic and encouraging, that it gave her all the validation she needed until she began sharing her poetry later in life.

At 19 with all her strength she stepped into sobriety and began to return to her true self. She also took up Ukidokan kickboxing, which supported her new path greatly. One of which being starting an arts company with her brother and a friend dedicated to giving a platform for independent artists to showcase their work, to where she read her first poem to an audience for their first event. Later moving on to read at various events with all of the courage she could gather, in spite of her fear of public speaking. Owing to the fact that she knew how poetry and art saved her life, she felt compelled to pay it forward because of her newfound vitality in sobriety.

She came to a crossroads in yearning to join the various parts of herself that she felt was in stark contrast to the seed of her spiritual nature. Ready to nurture, grow, and be. She had begun a yoga practice and later went on to teach, which gave her a peaceful foundation and new confidence in public speaking. Amidst her soul searching she found additional practices that aided in returning her to her center of peace. It was at this time in her early 20's that she went onto receive her Reiki Master certification.

In the thick of this condensed time she found herself reconnecting with her writing and for the first time knowing she needed to share her poetry with the world. Although it was quite the journey, she persevered to bring this poetry to you today.

She hopes to give back the gifts that the magic of words have bestowed upon her life so freely and that you may see and know the brilliance of them, in your own life, for all of your moments.

HOW THIS BOOK CAME TO BE

I have always believed in the magic of life and its wonder in each moment. And then there was a time that I became distanced from this knowing becoming swept up in the illusions of this world and chaos that life can sometimes bring. Poetry has always brought me back to my center. During a time of seeming lack of monetary means, I began to step outside and enjoy all of the riches that the earth gives to us freely with each sunrise, without expectation. The crispness of the air in the morning, the warmth of the sun on my skin, the comfort that trees solidly and tangibly give by simply being their regal selves. It was in these moments of returning to myself that I re-remembered the magic of my youth and my knowing of the divine spark that lives within all, connecting us, comforting me, consoling me, and creating space for me to grow just as nature does with gentle ease, yet always moving and changing, but still remaining all the same.

We are all surrounded and supported by the same Mother Earth. She saved me and listened to the voice of my heart when I felt there was no one else who I could speak to. In return she gave me her loving wisdom, simple & kind.

My wish is that with these poems, you may be connected to the knowing that Mother Earth is always here for you in every way. I hope that together with each of us knowing this completely with all of our being, with our roots connecting us, that we may honor Mother Earth wholeheartedly now and always in every way. Just the same as she does for us with each breath we get to take.

Thank you for opening this book and I pray that you may feel the magic of words as you read.

I

LETTERS FROM MOTHER EARTH

It is time and the world is ready to know what they mean to me, how much I love them. Unconditionally, yes unconditionally. Yes all is always in perfection & divine bliss is every moment. This truth is and ever shall be and remain.

It is all for you, humankind.

Love,
Mother Earth

1

TO HUMANKIND

Place your hand
upon me
as our heart beats
The blood running through
your veins
is the
humming of silence
still moving through
vibration
rest your head
I will soothe you
all one ever needs is one
true moment
to last a lifetime- 100 years
though the connection
is eternal

the human body
could use the touch
to touch
factor

Love,
Mother Earth to
Humankind

2

HANDFUL OF SKY

Pray I may sing a
song of silence
- to you.
So you may know
with certainty
that the air of the sky
sitting delicately
soft like silk
- upon your skin
is my breathe
-Pray you may feel
but a handful
of it
Seals a seed
for you to inhale
take within
to become the

fiber of cells
Saving me
the swaying of saying
to thee through sun & moon
of the mending
uncageable
song of silence

Love,
The Sky

3

LENGTH OF A THREAD

Know when I whisper
it is simply
another layer of
yourself
connecting to you
again
see the thread is only so
long in this life
know the more you
speak to me
the longer this
thread
becomes.

it is always as
you are ready
& need it to be.

Love,
Mother Earth

4

IT IS SO

When one knows
before they know
it is easy to almost
believe the voice
saying, "look about
-it is not so."
That is when one
must say,
"look within
-it is so."
This is how the
tree keeps track
of these things

because she knows
her roots are real
although one cannot
see them.

Love,
Mother Earth

5

I AM A CACTUS

I've lived as a cactus
for so long
You may see me in
a different setting
but the desert is
where I am
from & where
I belong
I will always be
a cactus.
Just as a wildflower
need be wild
we all have our
place in Mother Earth
I may appear guarded
I may not be
plentiful or

provide shade
but when you are
alone
in the sands of the desert
I will give you solace
all the same
I am a cactus & I
have my place on
Mother Earth.
as you do.

Love,
The Cactus

6

WAYS OF LOVE

When a seed is planted
it needs to be
left alone
in the soil with the earth
yes, it may be watered
and tended.
nurtured
but if we dig the earth
to check
on the seed
the roots will lose
their place
and need to start over

It is the seeds choice
whether to grow and be
or not be
This is the Way of Love.

Love,
Mother Earth

7

SHAMAN, THE SEED

how might I
tend to the seed
of our love.
roots in
the soil
of Mother Earth.
It's so much
more than that
It's the worm that
loosens the soil
It's the grass that
attracts the
animals
to nurture
us
It's the rain from
the heavens

from the rain dance
of the Shaman

that knows of the
seed below
because of her
talking to the land
and the trees and
the soil
and listening
She was born of a seed
of love
too
in the same.
Fractions
of a whole
each a note to
a symphony

Love,
The Seed

8

ROSEBUD

I see the flower
in bloom

and I smile
because I know
the blooming is
as beautiful
& mystifying
as its full bloom

know this as you bloom.

The eternal rose is
as sacred

as the eternal rosebud

Love,
Mother Earth

9

I AM HERE FOR YOU

I am here for you
to plant your
seeds
and watch them grow
and let them nourish
you
I am here for you
to walk on
and have a ground
and place to be to
connect with humans
I am here for you
to build upon
and manifest your dreams
and structure your
creativity
I am here for you

to return to me
and when you grow tired
and when your work is
through
I am here for you

I am
the dirt of the
Earth

Love,
The Dirt

II

LOVE LETTERS

10

SULENATANA

The moon of the night is soft and my heart is heavy
from the tears I hold inside

Loneliness, disappointment from my own
expectation......and a tethered mask of trying to hide it

I take this mask off before I come to you like a servant
before her Queen- my heart is beating- barely in my
chest- ready to leave once it has the key

I have no one and no one has me

Soles of my feet connect to your holy ground and so my soul feels relief

I bow at your feet, kneel over as a beggar for a blessing and you lift me from within to hold you and know you

I pour into you and you into me- my tears release, my heart is joined with yours and yours with mine.

My breath is now your breath and so long as I remember this I will always know this peace.

This is what I know from hugging you

I am yours forever, Sulenatana

Love,
Racquel

11

YOU ARE PERFECT IN MY EYES

I see you and
I can be- the only
hand you ever
need to hold.
because I have hands
you cannot see.
You are perfect in my
eyes
crying with all that
you are
broken in pieces
I see you and
I can feel all of
what you will be
because it is only
when you have
nothing

that you can be
everything
that you are
everything
and
nothing
in one
the colors this creates
is only seen
when one hears with
their heart
and sees with their
soul
You are perfect in
my eyes
I see you and
I can be the only hand
you ever need to hold
because I have hands
you cannot see
I am yours forever,
RACQUEL

Love,
Sulenatana

12

MEDITATION

I am grateful
when I need you all
I need to do is look
out my window
and there you are
It is all too circular
that it should be
all I need do is
open my heart
to receive your love

Love,
Racquel

13

NORTH STAR

When you saw me tonight
It made me very happy
I see you all the time
You live your life
and go about
Then the sun sets
and when I am lucky
and you stroll the
night
on a clear sky
when you breathe
long enough
to look up and see
me
it makes me smile.
Any wish you hold in
your heart

tell me and I will
make it yours
You will know when
it comes true
how much I Love You
and because I do not
have hands
and arms
to hold you
to touch you
You will know that
I do
when it comes true
when you saw me tonight
it made me
very happy
you always do

Love,
North Star

14

CLEAR NIGHT SKY, CLEAR MIND

Today it wasn't raining
for the first night
in a few days
Bettie & Ringo are always
ecstatic every
time we go
for a walk
or anywhere
The crisp of the air
is so clean
and fresh
to breathe in, to exhale
is like medicine
Then we come near
the end of our
stroll
I look to the sky and I

see you shining
You captivate me
Your blessing encircles
me.
I remember to make a
wish
It's like I felt you
looking at me
and I was still enough
to feel it
and look up
Thank You for looking
after me
Thank You for loving
me
While I learn to love
myself.

Love,
Racquel

15

MEDITATION

I AM THE INFINITE
THE INFINITE IS ME
WE ARE ONE
I AM ONE WE ARE ALL

16

AIR

I heard you
with my heart today
when I went to a
closed off corner to cry
in private
I took my breathes
deep breathe in <-----
deep breathe out ----->
deep breathe in <-----
deep breathe out ----->
I didn't know I
needed to cry so
until I did
that's when I heard
you with my
heart
I simply had the

answer
to my every question
And I had enough
calm
left within me
to walk out with
dignity & grace
because I heard you
with my heart today
from breathing in &
breathing out

Love,
Racquel

17

BUNDLED AS A BABY

I knew you needed me
today
your Heart cried out
to me
She was weary & weak
I entered upon your
breathe
completely to go to
your Heart
and save Her
I had you exhale
deeply to release
and let go
of the cactus needles
you had clung
so long &
plucked them out

although it may
pulse for a bit
I promise it is only better now.
I covered you as a
blanket
bundled as a baby
so you would be
able to
walk out
with dignity and grace
that you are.
I am always here for
you
please remember when
you breathe
in_and_out
that I Love You

Love,
The Air

18

MEDITATION

I woke up this morning
to birds singing
a chorus of them
singing a symphony
for me.
the morning after I put one foot
in front of the
other.
I know I did the right
thing.

19

FLYING & SUCH

This is an odd space
of not knowing what
to do
All of the stages I had
built to feel
safe
I've given away
in doing so it feels
I've released enough
anchors
to begin to rise
into a space I
feel only partially
accustomed to
partially because I feel
free
and that freedom grants

my heart
a solidness so
spear-like
I can pierce through
anything.
It's either sleeping too
much
or too little
This new space will take
some time
I trust in You all the same.

Love,
Racquel

20

MY CHILD

You know child
You are a traveler
always learning
always seeking
learners are seekers anyways
and those who seek & learn
are travelers
This is the way it is to
always be
The womb of the Mother
is safe & warm
the child must be
borne

You are always in my womb
when you love

because all you seek is within
that

Love,
Mother Earth

21

MEDITATION

There is a Tree for
every person
like a Guardian Angel.

22

I WALK TO YOU

I do believe as I breathe
more bonded to you
I become
I feel my back against
your bark
I am strengthened
I feel solid
as if your bark
is now my back
and I can do anything
and be anything
and have peace
while being
I rest my hands
to touch you
like you are holding
them

any angst, any anxiety
I held before I came
here
has dissipated
Now it is only us.
my path is clear
because trees grow
where there is space
for them.

Love,
Racquel

23

I AM HERE

When you rest your back
against my bark
I am strengthening you
to be solid within
so my bark
may be your back
you can do anything
you can be anything
be peace
while being
When you rest your hands
to touch me
I am holding them
Release all that you came
to me with
So I may fill you with
infinity

that is US.
Now the path is clear
for you to grow.

I Love You Child.

Love,
Mother Safara

24

MEDITATION

I smell the moist of the
Earth
as if it were Spring.

25

PICNIC

Sun is setting
Air is warm & cool
Moon is glowing, to
my right
already.
Birds are chirping
in the trees
blanket beneath me
picnic before me
Wind gently flowing from
my right to left
I wonder what you think
when I am afar
from you.
if you think of me
what you think of me when it seems the day takes you
from me

Then I look at the flowers
sprouting from the grass
and I suppose it's
one in the same.
When I am stuck inside
I dream & yearn
for it all
the same.
(the wind whispers)
Be calm
be still
be open
be one
Be with me

Love,
Racquel

26

ELEMENTS

I will bring elements
to you
to enjoy
Air, Moon, Birds
As you enjoy your picnic on your blanket
My Love penetrates
through all things
in all times
state of mind
state of being
varying- moment to moment
vibration of unconditional
unwavering
calm
still
open

oneness
be

Love,
Mother Earth

27

MOTHER SAFARA

THE TREE ON MY WALKING PATH THAT STARTED IT ALL

as I sit beneath you
at your feet
whispers of the ages
you breathe
into me
the love which becomes
me
solidifies and wholeness
is now that
I am
I rest my head
upon you
you were made for me
and I for you

Love,
Racquel

28

FIGURE EIGHT

When the mind
is still from
perplexion
I am able to
bless you with
infinity

And you see
because you
do not know
you are free
to be still
when the mind
is perplexed.

Love,
Mother Safara

29

MEDITATION

The wind is not visible
to the eye it is
transparent. Yet it is
still felt when it brushes
upon you and is mighty
to uproot trees create
storms and is the reason
for our breathing among
other things. The wind
is much like love.

BONUS POEMS

To show our gratitude for your support of the launch of Wild Horses Press and Racquel TW's first poetry book, we'd like to offer these 11 bonus poems written by Racquel, from our heart to yours.

III

FOR YOU, MY CHILD

LOVE, GOD

30

THIS MORNING AND ALWAYS

Hello Creator
I come before you this morning
With a humble head
I bow down
Before you
I know I am cluttered
I know I am well many things
But truly I come before you
Letting all of this go
That I may be of complete service to you
To humankind, to Mother Earth
I know I need to rest more each day
I know I need to let go of all the
Achieving and accomplishment
That I seek
All I need seek is you
And all is accomplished and achieved in that

I come before you this morning
Willing to let go of everything
Which stands in the way
Of my service to you
With a humble head
I bow down
Before you
Here is my heart
Here is my head
Here I am
I can feel the fear trembling within me
I am ready to step into all that I may be
This morning and always

Love,
Racquel

31

SOW LOVE AND REAP LOVE

Sew love and reap love
Plant kindness and receive kindness
Keep your pure heart steadfast
And I will always hear your prayers
And hold you when you cry
Allow me to soften your heart
So that you will know
By letting me into it
That will be the most courageous
Thing you will ever do
Breathing even when you are scared to
Because you trust in the strength
Of my love
That can do all things
Yield all things of the pure heart
Sleep peacefully my child

With this knowing
That you can let go
And still hold everything you need

Love,
God

32

NOTHING

Give yourself time
Everyday
To sit and think about
Nothing

Love,
God

33

ONE BREATH

If you could see the brightness and brilliance
Of your very being
Perhaps then
You would believe me
And all that is already in your name
All that is your birthright
With no task nor deed to be done
To receive them
Simply receive it
Let go and be it
To know what you cannot see
With thine eyes
But feel in thy heart
That is one of the greatest lessons of this life
To feel all of the beauty of the unseen
And see the truth of its tangibility
So thick that one could

Slice through it with a knife if desired
The brightness and brilliance
Of your very being
Is all of the heavens
In one body
That is why so many seek to steal it
Know that I am here for you
To protect you
To guide you
To remind you
Of all that you are
Of all that you hold
In one breathe
And if for some reason
It is too hard to remember
And this world makes you too sad
Here I am
For you to return to
On your last breath

Love,
God

34

MY CHILD, MY MOON

In the dark of the night
I am with you my child
One day all the pieces will
Come together
This I promise- completely
In your heart
There are many a great treasures
Keep them in your chest for know
You will know when it is your time
To open your heart and shine
With all that you are.
In the meantime
You are all that you need be and more
For all time you are
In the dark of the night
The moon
Yes, the moon my child

For all the world
You shine
And the moon with all her own darkness
On display
Still illuminates
Just the same
In the dark of the night
I am
Always
With you
My child
My moon

Love,
God

35

THIS IS ME

In the darkness
There I am
In the bright shining sun
There I am
In the pain
There I am
In the forgiveness
There I am
In the whisper of your heart
There I am
In the roar of your lioness call
There I am
In all the in between
In all the nothing
Close your eyes and look inside
All the world within you
All the worlds within you

They all exist for you
They all exist because of you
Let me serve you
As you so serve me
Here you are
And here I am
This is me

Love,
God

36

CLOSE YOUR EYES

I could chant
How perfect you are
For all of my life
All of your life
And it would still bear repeating
Wrap you in the sweetness of spring
But my love winter still does exist
You are perfect
You are perfect
You are perfect
Stand in stillness
Take the air in and
And
And
Well close your eyes
And let me show you in your heart
Do you? Do you notice?

Keep breathing
There
There my child
Here am I always
I could chant
For all of my life
For all of your life
Just as the birds will always sing
So will I
My love for you
Let me show you
Well close your eyes

Love,
God

37

STILLNESS OF SILENCE

In the stillness of silence
You will know me
In the quiet of breathe
There I am
Do you feel fearful in the strength of spirit?
To feel the smallness
Yet grandeur of the world in your heart
I know it's hard to see the tired in your eyes
Lay your head to rest Upon my shoulder child
Close your eyes knowing you are safe in my arms
Just as you have always been
In spite of what the world does bring
I have always held you
Those times that were so hard
That I whisked you away
From your body
Until you were ready to return

One day it will all make sense
Strange and puzzling as it is
Know that I love you
Thank you for forgiving me
In the unknowing
Of these evils
In the stillness of silence
You know me
In the quiet of breathe
I am

Love,
God

38

SACRED SKIN

Your skin is sacred
My sweet child
Let all who cross your path
Revel in the depth of your color
The richness of your soul
The gravity of the history
And story of survival
Thriving in your dna
Your ancestors sing and dance
Here in heaven
With the joy of knowing
That it all was worth it
Because of where you stand
And that is all
By the breath that you take
That is all
Nothing to prove or be

Besides being
Just you as you are
So know
as you look at your hands
as you look into your eyes
That every fiber of who
You are
My child
Is sacred

Love,
God

39

YOU ARE LOVED

My love my love my love my love
Deep breathe
To hear the water falling outside
The silence of all the moon brings
When your thoughts are still dancing
I hope you can
Take a deep breathe
Just for the sake of taking a deep breathe
With all the layers of action and accomplishment
I hope you can
Truly love yourself
For all that you are
For all that you are not
For all that you can be
For all that you cannot be
Deep breathe
I know the tension that brings

But
My love my love my love my love
Deep breathe
You are loved you are love you are loved you are loved
As you are as you are as you are as you are

Love,
God

40

EVERYTHING

Do you know what makes you special?

EVERYTHING

Always remember that

Love,
Mother Earth

THANK YOU

Thank you all so very much from the very depths of my soul. I thank you and I am grateful to you for reading my debut book. I compiled these poems in a very trying time in my early 20s, and it was put on my heart to publish it and put it out there for the world.

I believe that others may benefit from hearing the messages of unconditional love that Mother Earth so freely gave to me in some of my most trying times.

I pray that they bless you. All Glory To God.

If you got something from this book, please share it with someone that you care for who could benefit from it, and perhaps could use the message of Mother Earth's love. I look forward to staying connected with you all.

Many Blessings,

Racquel TW

CONNECT: RACQUEL TW

Racquel Tw
https://www.RacquelTW.com

Podcast "Spiritual Tools for Daily Living"
is available on Spotify and Apple Podcasts

INSTAGRAM: @Racquel_TW

YOUTUBE: Racquel TW

PINTEREST: @RacquelTW

TWITTER: @Racquel_TW

FOR INQUIRIES: WildHorsesPress@gmail.com

CONNECT: SPIRITUAL TOOLS SHOPPE

http://SpiritualToolsShoppe.com

INSTAGRAM: @SpiritualToolsShoppe

CONNECT: WILD HORSES PRESS

https://www.WildHorsesPress.com

INSTAGRAM: @WildHorsesPress

FOR INQUIRIES: WildHorsesPress@gmail.com

www.ingramcontent.com/pod-product-compliance
Lightning Source LLC
Chambersburg PA
CBHW021449070526
44577CB00002B/327
9781954539020